Indeed, many towns and cities on the Great Ocean Road were established early in
the history of Melbourne and provided a vital sea link for food, timber and other rural commod

Overseas shipping along this coastline was also central to settlement and development.
The first landfall on the Australian coast for cargo and immigrant ships bound for Melbourne was usually
Cape Otway, with the Cape Otway lighthouse being built in 1848 to aid navigation.

Both before and after the lighthouse was built, however, many shipwrecks occurred along this
coast and although tragic in themselves provide yet another fascinating insight into the history, character and
abundant diversity of the Great Ocean Road.

## Queenscliff

As a town, Queenscliff retains much of its
historic 19th century charm and atmosphere.
It has many historically and architecturally
significant buildings, particularly hotels which
made it a popular seaside resort in the 1880s
when coastal steamers regularly plied the waters
of Port Philip Bay from Melbourne.

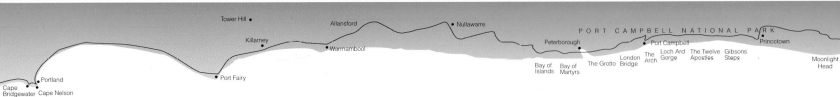

Cape Bridgewater · Cape Nelson · Portland · Port Fairy · Killarney · Warrnambool · Tower Hill · Allansford · Nullawarre · Bay of Islands · Bay of Martyrs · The Grotto · London Bridge · The Arch · Peterborough · Port Campbell · Loch Ard Gorge · The Twelve Apostles · Gibsons Steps · Princetown · PORT CAMPBELL NATIONAL PARK · Moonlight Head · Cape Otway · Melba Gully State Park · Lavers Hill · Triplet, Beauchamp, Hopetoun Falls · Mait's R (Rainforest) · OTWAY NATIONAL PARK · Johanna · Camping R

**The Ozone Hotel**

The Ozone Hotel, classified by the National Trust, was built in 1881 for James George Baillieu. It was named Ozone in 1886 after the famous paddle steamer of the same name.

The Ozone, the Grand Hotel and the Queenscliff Hotel (1887) reflected the grandiose building style of the economic boom decade of the 1880s in Victoria.

Queenscliff Historical Society

**Grand Hotel**, Queenscliff was built in 1881 and destroyed by fire in 1927. This photograph was taken in 1923 at the Catholic Federation Picnic. Vue Grand now stands in place of the Grand.

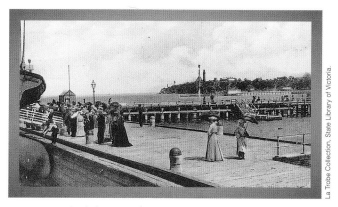

La Trobe Collection, State Library of Victoria.

Arriving on the steamer circa 1910. Today a modern car and passenger ferry operates from Sorrento to Queenscliff.

Shortland Bluff - Black Lighthouse -
60pdr Cannon on Cliff Top - Customs Boat Shed - Circa. 1875

Historic boat sheds

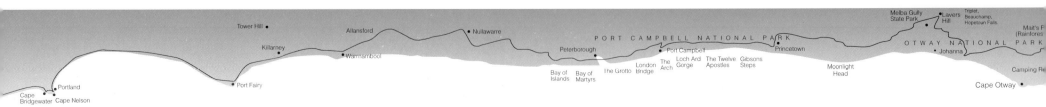

Queenscliff Hotel 1887

Fort Queenscliff with its black lighthouse is Australia's largest and best preserved military fortress dating back to the 1860s and the Crimean War. The fort was strategically located to protect the entrance to Port Phillip Bay.

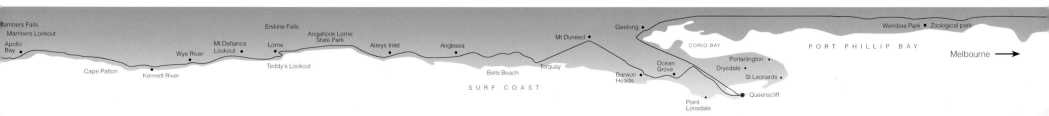

Point Lonsdale Lighthouse (1902) stands as an imposing sentinel to safeguard shipping across the treacherous
1,200 metre stretch of water known as the "Rip" between Point Lonsdale and Point Nepean. All shipping heading into Port Phillip Bay
bound for Geelong or Melbourne must pass safely through the Rip.

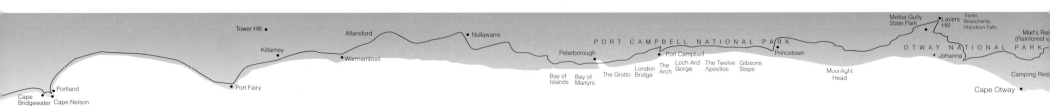

## Geelong

### *The Lightning*

In 1869, the Lightning, a famous Black Ball Line clipper ship on the Australian run, was destroyed by fire in Corio Bay while loading wool.

In 1854 the Lightning under its captain James "Bully" Forbes had set a Liverpool - Melbourne - Liverpool record never equalled for sailing ships of 5 months and 21 days (77 days to Australia and 63 days return - including 20 days in Hobson's Bay).

The Lightning also had the dubious honour of introducing a batch of 24 British wild rabbits to Australia in 1859 - to become the worst single pest to farmers in this country.

Artist Jack Spurling
Marwick and Paulig Ltd, London

La Trobe Collection, State Library of Victoria.

**SURF COAST**

riners Falls
Marriners Lookout
pollo
ay
Cape Patton
Kennett River
Wye River
Mt Defiance Lookout
Erskine Falls
Lorne
Teddy's Lookout
Angahook Lorne State Park
Aireys Inlet
Anglesea
Bells Beach
Torquay
Mt Duneed
Barwon Heads
Ocean Grove
Point Lonsdale
Queenscliff
St Leonards
Drysdale
Portarlington
CORIO BAY
Geelong
Werribee Park ■ Zoological park
PORT PHILLIP BAY
Melbourne →

Torquay is the heart of the Surf Coast. Indeed, the town's entire economy revolves around surfing with various surfing industry brand names prominent. Here are manufactured and sold surf boards, wetsuits, swimwear and other surfing accessories.

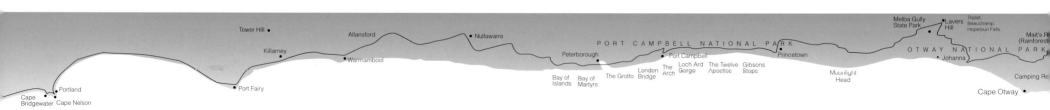

Sunny Garcia winning the Rip Curl Pro 2000 at Bells Beach (Surfing Victoria)

Surfing at Torquay. A series of spectacular ocean beaches from Ocean Grove and Barwon Heads to Torquay, Anglesea and Aireys Inlet make up what is known as the Surf Coast. Torquay and Bells Beach are world renowned surf beaches and in Easter of each year Bells Beach is the location of both national and international carnivals.

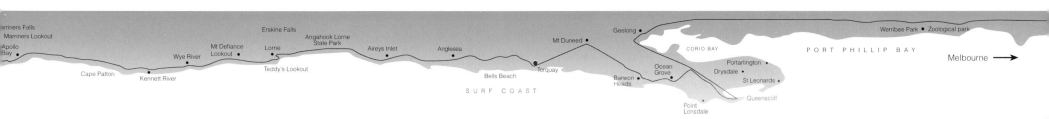

**Aireys Inlet**

Aerial view of the coast
at Aireys Inlet showing
Split Point Lighthouse
(constructed 1891) and
Eagle Rock.

Tower Hill

Allansford

Nullawarre

Killarney

Warrnambool

Peterborough

PORT CAMPBELL NATIONAL PARK

Melba Gully
State Park

Lavers
Hill

Triplet,
Beauchamp,
Hopetoun Falls.

Mait's Re
(Rainforest

OTWAY NATIONAL PARK

Port Campbell

Princetown

Johanna

Bay of
Islands

Bay of
Martyrs

The Grotto

London
Bridge

The
Arch

Loch Ard
Gorge

The Twelve
Apostles

Gibsons
Steps

Moonlight
Head

Camping Re

Portland

Port Fairy

Cape
Bridgewater

Cape Nelson

Cape Otway

The majestic sweep of the Surf Coast between Anglesea and Aireys Inlet
presents an enticing panorama.

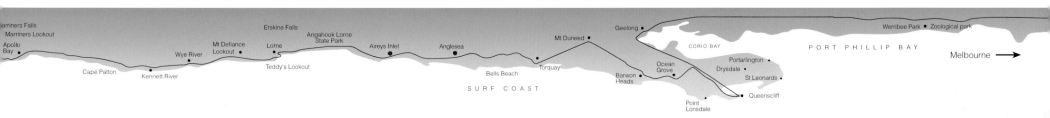

Marriners Falls
Marriners Lookout
Erskine Falls
Angahook Lorne
State Park
Geelong
Werribee Park ■ Zoological park
Apollo
Bay
Mt Defiance
Lookout
Lorne
Aireys Inlet
Anglesea
Mt Duneed
CORIO BAY
PORT PHILLIP BAY
Wye River
Ocean
Grove
Portarlington
Melbourne →
Cape Patton
Teddy's Lookout
Torquay
Drysdale
Kennett River
Bells Beach
Barwon
Heads
St Leonards
Point
Lonsdale
Queenscliff
SURF COAST

Lorne

Lorne. The coach for Birregurra outside the Lorne Post Office circa 1910.

Lorne – Great Ocean Road – "Marine Parade" circa 1930.

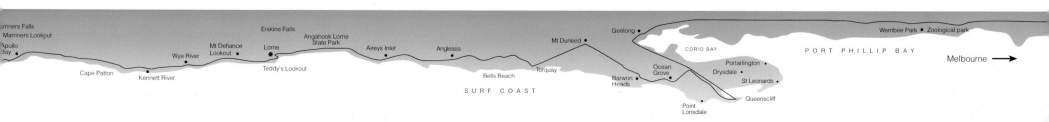

Lorne Historical Society

Timber Milling. Anglesea, Aireys Inlet, Lorne, Wye River, Kennett River and Apollo Bay were all first settled by loggers who arrived after the completion of Cape Otway lighthouse in 1848. Wooden tramways using winches or horses were used for transporting timber between forest and jetties.

Erskine Falls, Lorne.

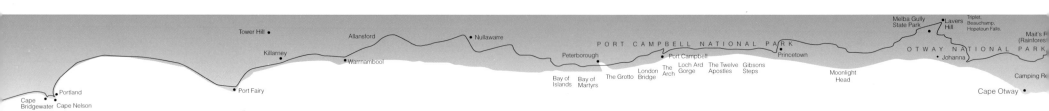

Tower Hill
Allansford
Nullawarre
Killarney
Warrnambool
Peterborough
Port Campbell
Bay of Islands
Bay of Martyrs
The Grotto
London Bridge
The Arch
Loch Ard Gorge
The Twelve Apostles
Gibsons Steps
PORT CAMPBELL NATIONAL PARK
Princetown
Moonlight Head
Melba Gully State Park
Lavers Hill
Triplet, Beauchamp, Hopetoun Falls.
OTWAY NATIONAL PARK
Johanna
Mait's R (Rainfores
Camping R
Cape Bridgewater
Cape Nelson
Portland
Port Fairy
Cape Otway

**Lorne Beach**

Lorne (pop 1,000) was first settled in 1853 and is a popular tourist and holiday destination. Situated on the coast in the midst of the Angahook - Lorne State Park it provides a wide range of activities for holiday-makers

Marriners Falls
Marriners Lookout
Apollo
Bay

Cape Patton

Kennett River

Wye River

Mt Defiance
Lookout

Teddy's Lookout

Erskine Falls

Lorne

Angahook Lorne
State Park

Aireys Inlet

Anglesea

Bells Beach

Torquay

Barwon
Heads

Point
Lonsdale

Ocean
Grove

Mt Duneed

Geelong

CORIO BAY

Queenscliff

Drysdale

St Leonards

Portarlington

Werribee Park ■ Zoological park

PORT PHILLIP BAY

Melbourne →

SURF COAST

Lorne Historical Society

Lorne Historical Society

Great Ocean Road from Teddy's Lookout, Lorne.

The Great Ocean Road between Lorne and Apollo Bay was carved into the southern coastal slopes of the Otway Ranges
by returned servicemen from World War I. Work was begun in 1918 and the road officially opened on 26 November, 1932.
A memorial plaque reads: This road was built to commemorate the services of sailors and soldiers in the Great War.

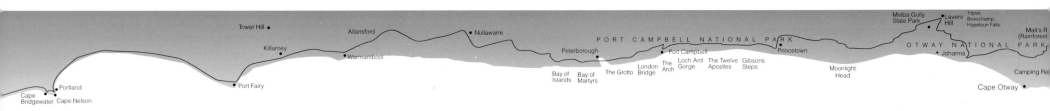

arriners Falls
Marriners Lookout
Erskine Falls
Geelong
Werribee Park ▪ Zoological park
Apollo
Bay
Angahook Lorne
State Park
Mt Duneed
CORIO BAY
PORT PHILLIP BAY
Wye River
Mt Defiance
Lookout
Lorne
Aireys Inlet
Anglesea
Portarlington
Melbourne →
Cape Patton
Kennett River
Teddy's Lookout
Bells Beach
Torquay
Ocean
Grove
Barwon
Heads
Drysdale
St Leonards
Queenscliff
Point
Lonsdale
SURF COAST

View of the Great Ocean Road coastline from Mt Defiance between Lorne and Wye River.

Kennett River

Aerial photographs of the Great Ocean Road between Kennett River
and Apollo Bay.

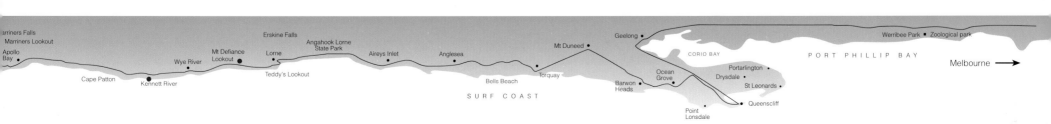

**Apollo Bay "Paradise by the Sea"**
is a popular holiday and tourist resort.

Tower Hill

Allansford

Nullawarre

Melba Gully
State Park

Lavers
Hill

Triplet,
Beauchamp,
Hopetoun Falls.

PORT CAMPBELL NATIONAL PARK

Mait's R
(Rainforest

Killarney

Peterborough

Port Campbell

Princetown

OTWAY NATIONAL PARK

Warrnambool

Port Campbell

Johanna

Bay of
Islands

Bay of
Martyrs

The Grotto

London
Bridge

The
Arch

Loch Ard
Gorge

The Twelve
Apostles

Gibsons
Steps

Moonlight
Head

Camping Re

Port Fairy

Cape Otway

Portland

Cape
Bridgewater

Cape Nelson

Fishing Fleet at Apollo Bay.

Apollo Bay Historical Society

The Great Ocean Road, Apollo Bay in the 1930s
(known then as Collingwood Street)

Marriners Falls, Apollo Bay

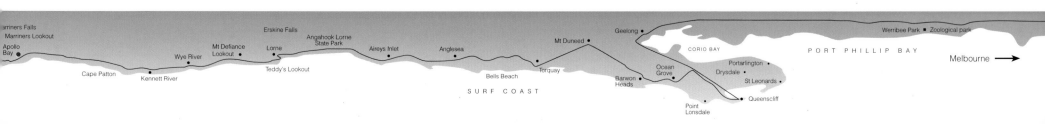

The coastal steamer, Casino, made about 2,500 trips along the coast between 1882 and 1932 before capsizing and sinking in heavy seas in Apollo Bay with the loss of 10 lives.

La Trobe Collection State Library of Victoria

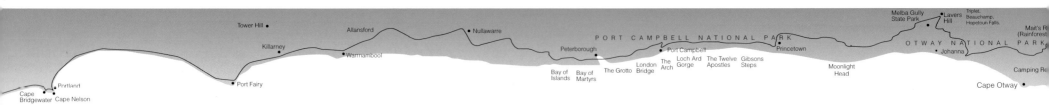

Apollo Bay Historical Society

APOLLO BAY, VICTORIA.

Historical photograph of Apollo Bay showing the old pier extending
out into the bay.  Apollo Bay pier was built in 1892 and was over 1500 feet in
length. The pier lasted until 1956 when the breakwater was built.

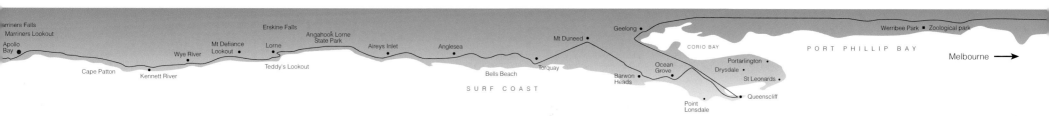

Mait's Rest provides a magnificent 45 minute walk in cool temperate rainforest.  Located in the Otway National Park
between Apollo Bay and Lavers Hill, Maits Rest has both walking tracks and boardwalks to assist visitors.
A centuries old Myrtle Beech tree is a feature of the walk while above the main ridge can be found huge Mountain Ash and Manna Gum eucalypts.

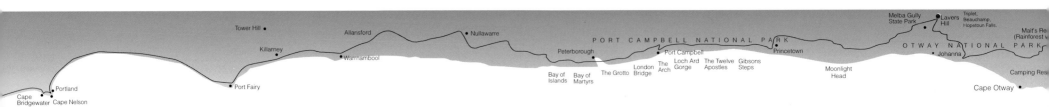

# THE GREAT OCEAN ROAD

### Beauchamp Falls

The beautiful Beauchamp Falls, deep in the heart of the Otway Ranges between Apollo Bay and Lavers Hill.

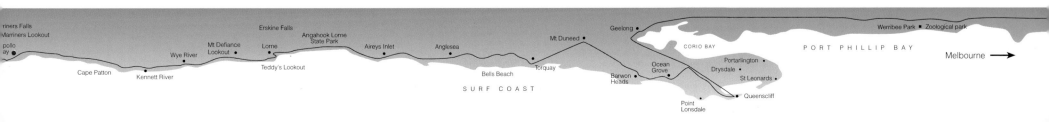

riners Falls
Marriners Lookout
pollo
ay

Cape Patton

Kennett River

Wye River

Mt Defiance
Lookout

Lorne

Teddy's Lookout

Erskine Falls

Angahook Lorne
State Park

Aireys Inlet

Anglesea

Bells Beach

SURF COAST

Torquay

Mt Duneed

Barwon
Heads

Point
Lonsdale

Ocean
Grove

Queenscliff

St Leonards

Drysdale

Portarlington

Geelong

CORIO BAY

PORT PHILLIP BAY

Werribee Park ■ Zoological park

Melbourne →

Cape Otway was usually the first landfall on the
Australian coast for overseas ships sailing to Melbourne.
The lighthouse on Cape Otway was built in 1848
as an essential aid to navigation. In 1835 the convict ship,
Neva, had seen only 22 survivors from 241 passengers
and crew when it had lost its way and hit a reef
off the northern tip of King Island.
In 1845 the emigrant ship, Cataraqui, had struck a
reef off the southern tip of King Island with only
9 survivors from 408 passengers and crew.

The barquentine Speculant was a trading vessel sailing from Portland to
Melbourne when she ran aground at Cape Patton on 10 February, 1911.

Eighteen sailing ships - both cargo and passenger - were wrecked on or near the
Great Ocean Road coastline when reaching the end of long sea voyages to
Melbourne. More than 300 ships have been wrecked along this entire coastline.

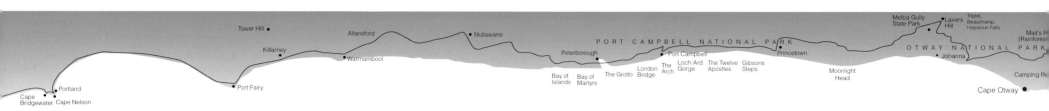

Marriners Falls
Marriners Lookout

Erskine Falls

Angahook Lorne
State Park

Geelong

Werribee Park  ■ Zoological park

Apollo
Bay

Mt Defiance
Lookout

Lorne

Aireys Inlet

Anglesea

Mt Duneed

CORIO BAY

PORT PHILLIP BAY

Melbourne →

Wye River

Portarlington

Cape Patton

Kennett River

Teddy's Lookout

Bells Beach

Torquay

Ocean
Grove

Drysdale

St Leonards

Barwon
Heads

Queenscliff

Point
Lonsdale

SURF COAST

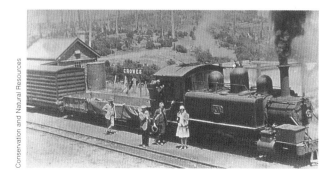

Conservation and Natural Resources

"The Beechy" shown here at Crowes, just south of Lavers Hill, was a narrow gauge train that ran between Colac, Beech Forestand Crowes (1902-1962) to provide settlers and the timber industry with an all weather access route to the Otways.

The beautiful Triplet Falls near Lavers Hill in the Otway Ranges.

Timber milling has been and remains a major industry for the Otway Ranges. The first inland mill was built near Forest in 1866.

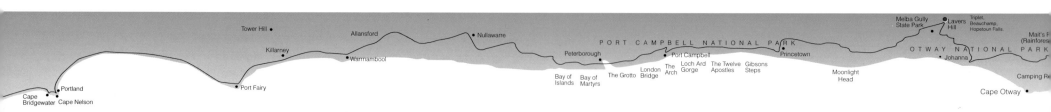

The Big Tree at Melba Gully, Lavers Hill, is a giant 300 year old Otway Messmate – a natural hybrid of Mountain Ash and Messmate.

Hopetoun Falls in the Otway Ranges.

**Flying Cloud**

The magnificent clipper ship
*Flying Cloud* by artist Jack Spurling.

*Gold Clippers* The discovery of gold in Australia
in 1851 saw a new and faster sailing ship on the
Australian run – the softwood "clipper" – mostly
built in North American shipyards.

The clipper ships of the 1850s represented
the pinnacle of sailing ship design: slender hulls,
graceful yacht-like bows and tall, rakish masts.
Clippers could carry over three acres of sail and
set record speeds that have never since been
equalled by sailing ships.

*The Great Circle Route* recognised
the world as spherical rather than rectangular
in shape. Sea captains could follow the arc of a
circle for a shorter journey and plunge as far as 55
degrees South into the Antarctic region before
turning north for Cape Otway. At such latitudes
clippers could also harness the furious ocean winds
and currents of the "Roaring Fifties".

With their capacity for great speed
clippers using the Great Circle Route could
often halve previous travelling times to Australia
to under 70 days and cut a thousand miles from
the journey. The record for the outward journey
by a clipper was 63 days and set
in 1854 by *James Baines*.

**Moonlight Head**
Anchors from the wrecks of the sailing ships Fiji (1891) and Marie Gabrielle (1869) can be seen at Moonlight Head.

Marriners Falls

Marriners Lookout

Apollo Bay

Cape Patton

Wye River

Kennett River

Mt Defiance Lookout

Lorne

Teddy's Lookout

Erskine Falls

Angahook Lorne State Park

Aireys Inlet

Anglesea

Bells Beach

Mt Duneed

Torquay

Barwon Heads

Ocean Grove

Point Lonsdale

Queenscliff

St Leonards

Drysdale

Portarlington

Geelong

CORIO BAY

Werribee Park ■ Zoological park

PORT PHILLIP BAY

Melbourne →

SURF COAST

## Moonlight Head

Awesome and thunderous
surf as waves crash
over the outer reef at
Moonlight Head.

Tower Hill •

Allansford •

• Nullawarre

Killarney •

Warrnambool •

PORT CAMPBELL NATIONAL PARK

Melba Gully
State Park

Lavers
Hill

Triplet,
Beauchamp,
Hopetoun Falls

Peterborough •

• Port Campbell

Princetown •

OTWAY NATIONAL PARK

Mait's R
(Rainforest

Bay of
Islands

Bay of
Martyrs

The Grotto

London
Bridge

The
Arch

Loch Ard
Gorge

The Twelve
Apostles

Gibsons
Steps

Moonlight
Head

Johanna •

Cape
Bridgewater

Portland

Cape Nelson

Port Fairy •

Cape Otway •

Camping Re

Flagstaff Hill Maritime Museum

The Rocket Line carried over a wreck.

This contemporary artist's sketch illustrates how a rocket line could be used to save survivors in a shipwreck. Such a line was fired to the Fiji at Moonlight Head on September 6, 1891. Despite this 11 crew members from a total crew of 26 drowned.

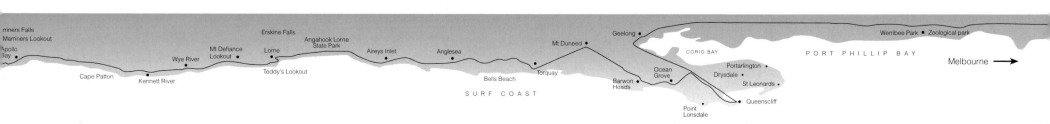

Dramatic limestone rock stacks form
the weathered remains of what were once
coastal headlands sculptured and eroded by
the sea over thousands of years.

Port Campbell National Park

# THE GREAT OCEAN ROAD

## Port Campbell National Park

Aerial photograph of the Great Ocean Road coastline near
Port Campbell showing Mutton Bird Island and Loch Ard Gorge.
Inset: A variety of fascinating limestone rock formations of the area with popular
names including "razorback" and "island arch".

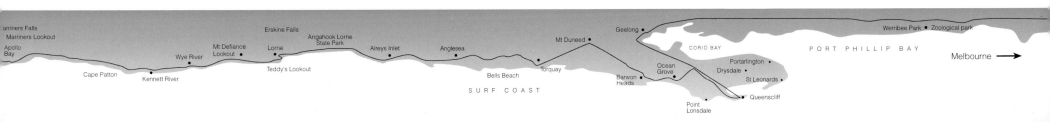

Gibson's Steps.
Romantic coastal imagery at Gibson's Steps near Port Campbell where limestone rock stacks combine with a beautiful
ocean sunset. The rock stacks have formed from the erosion of coastal headlands over thousands of years.

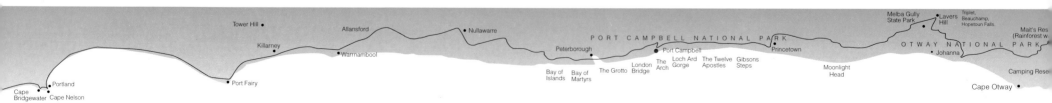

## The Twelve Apostles

The towering grandeur of this rock formation near Port Campbell holds a timeless fascination. Formed by the erosion of limestone headlands over thousands of years, the Twelve Apostles comprise one of Australia's most photographed natural features. A variety of moods and images can be seen under changing lighting and weather conditions.

Marriners Falls
Marriners Lookout

Apollo
Bay

Cape Patton

Kennett River

Wye River

Mt Defiance
Lookout

Teddy's Lookout

Lorne

Erskine Falls

Angahook Lorne
State Park

Aireys Inlet

Anglesea

Bells Beach

Torquay

Barwon
Heads

SURF COAST

Point
Lonsdale

Mt Duneed

Ocean
Grove

Queenscliff

Geelong

CORIO BAY

Portarlington

Drysdale

St Leonards

Werribee Park ■ Zoological park

PORT PHILLIP BAY

Melbourne →

The Twelve Apostles

Cape Bridgewater • Cape Nelson • Portland • Port Fairy • Killarney • Tower Hill • Warrnambool • Allansford • Nullawarre • Bay of Islands • Bay of Martyrs • The Grotto • Peterborough • London Bridge • The Arch • Loch Ard Gorge • Port Campbell • The Twelve Apostles • Gibsons Steps • PORT CAMPBELL NATIONAL PARK • Princetown • Moonlight Head • Melba Gully State Park • Lavers Hill • Triplet, Beauchamp, Hopetoun Falls. • Johanna • OTWAY NATIONAL PARK • Cape Otway • Mait's Rest (Rainforest) • Camping Res

Aerial view of the eroded
coastline of **Port Campbell**
**National Park.**

Marriners Falls
Marriners Lookout
Apollo
Bay
Cape Patton
Kennett River
Wye River
Mt Defiance
Lookout
Erskine Falls
Lorne
Teddy's Lookout
Angahook Lorne
State Park
Aireys Inlet
Anglesea
Bells Beach
Torquay
SURF COAST
Mt Duneed
Barwon
Heads
Ocean
Grove
Point
Lonsdale
Queenscliff
Geelong
CORIO BAY
Portarlington
Drysdale
St Leonards
Werribee Park ■ Zoological park
PORT PHILLIP BAY
Melbourne →

Port Campbell

Port Campbell Historical Society

Historical Port Campbell (circa 1920) showing the Ocean Beach Guest House, the Goods sheds and the Ladies Bathing Box.

Port Campbell - developed as a small fishing port with its first permanent settlers in the 1870s. In 1892 a rail link was made to Timboon enabling the town to become a holiday resort.
The opening of the Great Ocean Road in 1932 made the Port Campbell area a major tourist destination.

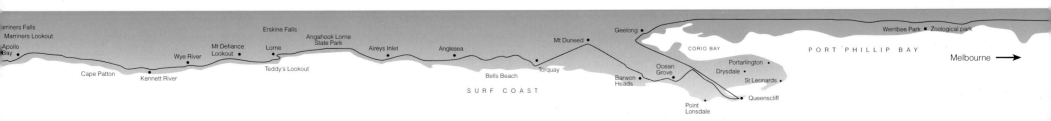

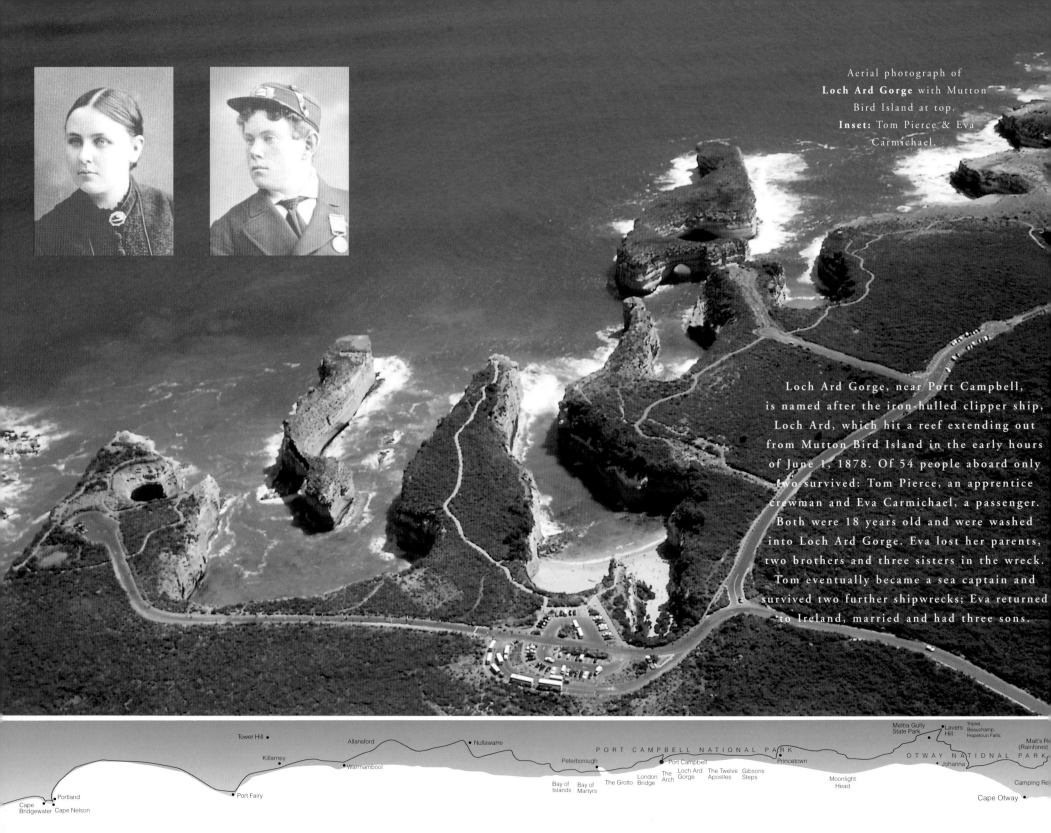

Aerial photograph of
**Loch Ard Gorge** with Mutton
Bird Island at top.
**Inset:** Tom Pierce & Eva
Carmichael.

Loch Ard Gorge, near Port Campbell,
is named after the iron-hulled clipper ship,
Loch Ard, which hit a reef extending out
from Mutton Bird Island in the early hours
of June 1, 1878. Of 54 people aboard only
two survived: Tom Pierce, an apprentice
crewman and Eva Carmichael, a passenger.
Both were 18 years old and were washed
into Loch Ard Gorge. Eva lost her parents,
two brothers and three sisters in the wreck.
Tom eventually became a sea captain and
survived two further shipwrecks; Eva returned
to Ireland, married and had three sons.

Tower Hill
Allansford
Nullawarre
Killarney
Warrnambool
Peterborough
Melba Gully State Park
Lavers Hill
Triplet, Beauchamp, Hopetoun Falls
PORT CAMPBELL NATIONAL PARK
OTWAY NATIONAL PARK
Mait's Re (Rainforest
Port Campbell
Princetown
Johanna
Bay of Islands
Bay of Martyrs
The Grotto
London Bridge
The Arch
Loch Ard Gorge
The Twelve Apostles
Gibsons Steps
Moonlight Head
Camping Re
Portland
Port Fairy
Cape Otway
Cape Bridgewater
Cape Nelson

A graphic contemporary illustration of the Loch Ard wreck from the Illustrated Sydney News of 1878.

Marriners Falls
Marriners Lookout
Apollo
Bay
Cape Patton
Kennett River
Wye River
Mt Defiance
Lookout
Erskine Falls
Lorne
Teddy's Lookout
Angahook Lorne
State Park
Aireys Inlet
Anglesea
Bells Beach
Torquay
Mt Duneed
Barwon
Heads
Ocean
Grove
Point
Lonsdale
Queenscliff
St Leonards
Drysdale
Portarlington
Geelong
CORIO BAY
Werribee Park ■ Zoological park
PORT PHILLIP BAY
Melbourne →

SURF COAST

## Port Campbell

The rugged coastline around Port Campbell
showing huge limestone cliffs rising dramatically
from sea level to heights of 70 metres.

Tower Hill •

Allansford

Killarney

• Nullawarre

Warrnambool

PORT CAMPBELL NATIONAL PARK

Melba Gully
State Park

• Lavers
Hill

Triplet,
Beauchamp,
Hopetoun Falls.

Peterborough

• Port Campbell

Princetown

OTWAY NATIONAL PARK

Mait's Re
(Rainforest

Port Fairy

Bay of
Islands

Bay of
Martyrs

The Grotto

London
Bridge

The
Arch

Loch Ard
Gorge

The Twelve
Apostles

Gibsons
Steps

Moonlight
Head

• Johanna

Camping Res

Cape
Bridgewater

• Portland

• Cape Nelson

Cape Otway

# THE GREAT OCEAN ROAD
## Port Campbell - Peterborough

**The Arch   The Grotto   London Bridge**
The limestone coastline around Port Campbell has been
sculptured by the sea over thousands of years to form a
range of grand and fascinating rock formations.
On January 15th, 1990 the landward arch of London Bridge
(left) collapsed leaving the present structure (right).

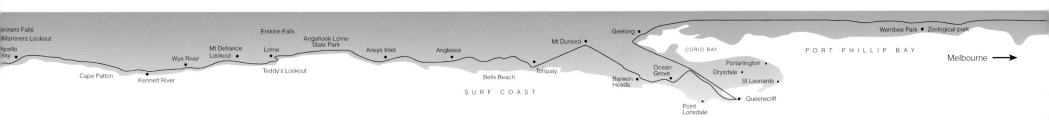

London Bridge

Bay of Martyrs

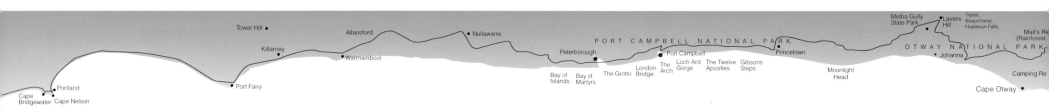

Tower Hill
Allansford
Nullawarre
PORT CAMPBELL NATIONAL PARK
Melba Gully
State Park
Lavers
Hill
Triplet,
Beauchamp,
Hopetoun Falls.
Killarney
Peterborough
Port Campbell
Princetown
OTWAY NATIONAL PARK
Mait's Re
(Rainforest
Warrnambool
Johanna
Bay of
Islands
Bay of
Martyrs
The Grotto
London
Bridge
The
Arch
Loch Ard
Gorge
The Twelve
Apostles
Gibsons
Steps
Moonlight
Head
Camping Re
Port Fairy
Portland
Cape
Bridgewater
Cape Nelson
Cape Otway

# Peterborough

## *The Schomberg*

Peterborough is the scene of another famous shipwreck - that of the luxurious clipper Schomberg (2,300 tons) on Boxing Day 1855. Captained by James "Bully" Forbes and on her maiden voyage Schomberg ran aground on a sand-covered reef about 300 yards from shore. The ship had been built at a cost of £43,000 and could boast a 400 volume library, velvet pile carpets, mahogany furniture and 60 staterooms.

Although no lives were lost and all passengers were taken off by a passing coastal steamer the loss of the Schomberg was scandalous.

La Trobe Collection: State Library of Victoria.

Under perhaps the most experienced sea captain of the time she had not only run aground in good weather and calm seas but at a point where she should have been 10 miles off the coast. At the time Forbes was reported to have been preoccupied below decks playing cards with a young female passenger and the ship's surgeon.

Forbes was placed on trial in Melbourne for negligence and although acquitted on the spurious grounds that the reef the Schomberg struck was uncharted, his reputation was left in ruins.

The Schomberg Artist Philip J. Gray

rriners Falls
Marriners Lookout
Apollo
Bay
Cape Patton
Kennett River
Wye River
Mt Defiance Lookout
Lorne
Teddy's Lookout
Erskine Falls
Angahook Lorne State Park
Aireys Inlet
Anglesea
Bells Beach
Torquay
Barwon Heads
Point Lonsdale
Mt Duneed
Ocean Grove
Queenscliff
Geelong
CORIO BAY
Portarlington
Drysdale
St Leonards
Werribee Park  ▪ Zoological park
PORT PHILLIP BAY
Melbourne →
SURF COAST

Hopkins River Boat Sheds, **Warrnambool** are classified by the National Trust and were built in three stages: 1885, 1887 and 1892.

TEA
OPEN

Melba Gully
State Park
Lavers
Hill
Triplet,
Beauchamp,
Hopetoun Falls.

Tower Hill
Allansford
Nullawarre
PORT CAMPBELL NATIONAL PARK
Mait's R
(Rainforest
Killarney
Peterborough
Port Campbell
Princetown
OTWAY NATIONAL PARK
Warrnambool
Johanna
Bay of
Islands
Bay of
Martyrs
The Grotto
London
Bridge
The
Arch
Loch Ard
Gorge
The Twelve
Apostles
Gibsons
Steps
Moonlight
Head
Camping Re
Port Fairy
Portland
Cape
Bridgewater Cape Nelson
Cape Otway

Lake Pertobe, Warrnambool, children's playground
with Lady Bay and pier at top.

Fletcher Jones Gardens, Warrnambool.

The town of Warrnambool was establised in 1847. It is now a large provincial city with approximately 26,000 people.
Its main industries are tourism, food processing and textiles.

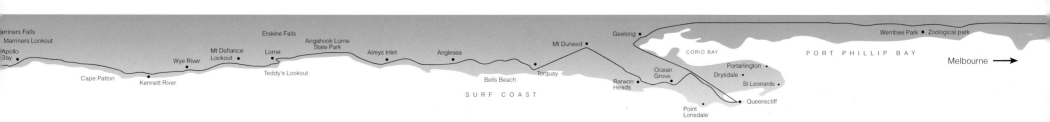

Warrnambool Historical Society

Liebig Street, Warrnambool circa 1927.

Warrnambool Historical Society

A contemporary view of Liebig Street, Warrnambool.

The Ozone Hotel, Warrnambool opened in 1890 and was another example of the grandiose archeticture of the economic boom decade of the 1880s.
The Ozone, which burnt down in 1929, stood on the site of the present day Warrnambool Hotel.

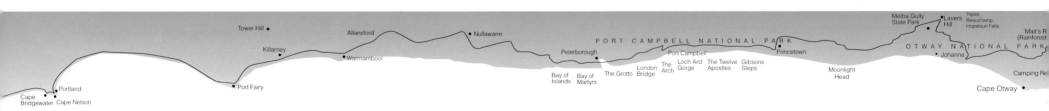

Flagstaff Hill recreates the atmosphere of an early Australian port.

Left: Porcelain peacock, 5 feet high and made by Mintons of England in 1851. The peacock was to have been shown at exhibition in Melbourne and Sydney in 1879 and 1880 but was washed ashore from the wreck of the Loch Ard in June 1878.

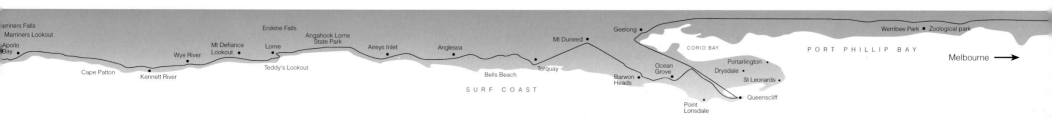

The picturesque Moyne River is at the heart of the **Port Fairy** township providing safe anchorage for both fishing boats and pleasure craft.

Cape Bridgewater
Cape Nelson
Portland
Port Fairy
Tower Hill
Killarney
Warrnambool
Allansford
Nullawarre
Peterborough
Bay of Islands
Bay of Martyrs
The Grotto
London Bridge
The Arch
Loch Ard Gorge
The Twelve Apostles
Gibsons Steps
Port Campbell
PORT CAMPBELL NATIONAL PARK
Princetown
Moonlight Head
Melba Gully State Park
Lavers Hill
Triplet, Beauchamp, Hopetoun Falls.
Johanna
OTWAY NATIONAL PARK
Mait's Re (Rainforest
Camping Re
Cape Otway

Port Fairy is a town of great historical charm with more than 50 buildings
classified by the National Trust.

The Western Victorian ports of Warrnambool, Port Fairy and Portland
were all established early in the settlement of Victoria as whaling and sealing bases.
Port Fairy developed into a busy coastal port exporting rural commodities to
Melbourne, Tasmania and directly to London.

**Cape Nelson Lighthouse, Portland** is yet another solitary white sentinel to both symbolise and characterise that which is the Great Ocean Road. Built in 1883 the lighthouse stands 24 metres tall and 76 metres above sea level. Its light has a range of 22 nautical miles.

Cape Bridgewater
Cape Nelson
Portland
Port Fairy
Killarney
Warrnambool
Tower Hill
Allansford
Nullawarre
Peterborough
Bay of Islands
Bay of Martyrs
The Grotto
London Bridge
The Arch
Loch Ard Gorge
The Twelve Apostles
Gibsons Steps
Port Campbell
Princetown
Moonlight Head
PORT CAMPBELL NATIONAL PARK
Melba Gully State Park
Lavers Hill
Triplet, Beauchamp, Hopetoun Falls.
Johanna
Cape Otway
OTWAY NATIONAL PARK
Mait's P (Rainfores
Camping Re

1. London Inn, 1844.
2. Town Hall, built in 1863 now serves as an historical
museum and genealogical research centre.
3. Customs House, 1849.
4. St. Stephens Church, 1856.

Portland was Victoria's first permanent settlement and
was founded by Edward Henty in 1834.  As many as 200 historic
buildings from the 1800s can be found in the city area.

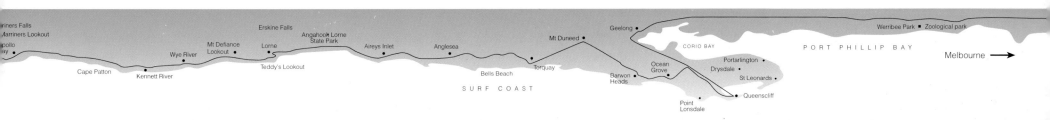

**The Blowholes, Cape Bridgewater, Portland**
Weathered volcanic rock at the base of these cliffs results in spectacular spouts of sea spray during heavy seas.

Tower Hill •

Melba Gully
State Park

Lavers
Hill

Triplet,
Beauchamp,
Hopetoun Falls

Allansford

• Nullawarre

PORT CAMPBELL NATIONAL PARK

OTWAY NATIONAL PARK

Mait's F
(Rainfores

Killarney

Peterborough

Port Campbell

Princetown

• Warrnambool

Loch Ard
Gorge

The Twelve
Apostles

Gibsons
Steps

• Johanna

Bay of
Islands

Bay of
Martyrs

The Grotto

London
Bridge

The
Arch

Moonlight
Head

Camping Re

• Portland

• Port Fairy

Cape Otway •

Cape
Bridgewater Cape Nelson